The
Victor
Poems

ALSO BY ANTHONY CALESHU

POETRY
Of Whales: in Print, in Paint, in Sea, in Stars, in Coin, in House, in Margins
The Siege of the Body and a Brief Respite

CRITICISM
Reconfiguring the Modern American Lyric: The Poetry of James Tate
Poetry and Public Language (co-edited with Tony Lopez)

FICTION
Churchtown: The Tale of Suzy Delou and Faye Fiddle (a novella)

Anthony Caleshu

The Victor Poems

Shearsman Books

First published in the United Kingdom in 2015 by
Shearsman Books
50 Westons Hill Drive
Emersons Green
BRISTOL
BS16 7DF

Shearsman Books Ltd Registered Office
30–31 St. James Place, Mangotsfield, Bristol BS16 9JB
(this address not for correspondence)

www.shearsman.com

ISBN 978-1-84861-431-4

ACKNOWLEDGEMENTS
Many thanks to Philip Coleman for discussions about this book
in manuscript. Some ideas and language are taken from
Aristotle, Emerson, Melville etc.; poem 11's title comes from
David Herd's *Enthusiast!* Cover art is by Thomas Barwick.
Grateful acknowledgement is made to the editors of the following
publications where *The Victor Poems* first appeared,
sometimes in different forms:

Poems 1, 2, 3, 4, 5 in *Boston Review*, as winner of
Boston Review Poetry Prize 2010, chosen by Peter Gizzi
Poems 6, 8, 10 in *New Walk*
Poems 7 and 11 in *Shearsman*
Poems 13, 15, 16, 17, 18 in *Web-Conjunctions*
Poem 20 in *Poetry Review*
Poems 12, 14, 21, 27, and 31 in *Narrative Magazine*
Poems 33, 34, 35 in *The Interpreter's House*
Poems 22 and 23 in *The Manchester Review,* reprinted
in *The Best British Poetry 2014* (Ed. Mark Ford)
Poems 28, 30 in *Denver Quarterly*
Poem 39 in *Salamander*

CONTENTS

I

II

For my family
For friends

We walk alone in the world. Friends such as we desire are dreams and fables. But a sublime hope cheers ever the faithful heart...

— Ralph Waldo Emerson

I.

1.

Victor, we say, where are you? The wind has a mind of its own.

It has corrupted the dogs who refuse to mush but sit lazily head in paws.

It has whipped the snow like a dairy treat but we are allergic to dairy.

Do not look us in the lips, which are chapped and cracked where our smiles used to be.

On account of our beards, our wives wouldn't kiss us – we wouldn't let them come with us.

We are now more alone than ever, and we've never been good at being alone: ask our bosses, our neighbors, our former amours.

A friend like you, especially in the fresh air, will always be a breath of fresh air.

We follow the horizon to where the blue of the sky meets the white of the ice.

It took turbulence for us to get here, and for us to get here to pick up our phones.

We cry to our wives, who cry to us, and so on.

We need to find you we know, but knowledge was never our goal.

We're the heroes of an empty drama: involving no
terrorists, nor crash landing.

We'd take comfort in Aurora Borealis, if there were any
Aurora Borealis.

We'd find joy in penguins, if there were any penguins.

Victor, we say… Victor, can you hear us! But there is no
response.

We tell ourselves about your pioneering ways with GPS
and GLONASS, even though our signal is weak, and we
are weaker.

2. Round after round

To be so many friends to so many people.

You've always been one of us even though you were
never one of us.

The last time we saw you… when was the last time we
saw you?

We'd all gone skiing in Canada, but you'd gone to Cancún
– the postcard read

See you soon.

We never saw you soon.

We looked to the moon while tuning our guitars.

It could have been the drugs – we were all on drugs – you
never did drugs.

There was the time you saved us from the guy whose
girlfriend had a guilty conscience.

There was the time you sponsored a Christmas Swim for
those of us who could not swim.

Somebody has to teach you, you said, pushing us cold and
deep into the wake of the lake – and that someone isn't
me.

For too long, you've avoided us.

Disappeared, just when the rest of us were trying to appear to the world.

Out of the lake we paddled, until we shivered on shore.

You were already, someone said, out the door.

For how long have we chased you – shot after shot at the bar?

Even *in absentia*, you put your credit card   down.

It's all paid for, the bartender said: round

        after round

  after round   after round

     after round.

3.

We'd blame you for this tour, if only this were a tour.

In you, we see the possibility of authority, white flecks
through a white beard.

> *When unions ground you, call Victor –*
> *Where weather prevents you, call Victor –*

We'd look for you in the trees in the air – if there were
any trees in the air.

The only air here is for polar bear and walrus.

To our chagrin, we are getting as thin as the air.

This sort of lean is no good for no-body.

Our heads are lost in blue skies, without even a broken
cloud.

We drift in high winds.

> *When melting occurs, call Victor –*
> *When war prevents you, call Victor –*

With our dogs on our backs, we cross this single season
of ice via snow-cats.

Fifteen kilometers of visibility and still we can't see
anything.

Short of cache positioning, short of personnel logistics,
we await you like a star across the sky.

We need re-supply.

Your breath is not our breath.

> *Breathe in Victor –*
> *Warm Victor –*

If there were trees, we'd be climbing them.

If there were trees, you'd welcome us within their white
globe of flowers.

4. *The hours go by like days*

The days go by like weeks.

The weeks go by like years.

And so on… and so on… and so:

       Once, you stole a coat.

Once, we stole a coat.

We stole it because we were cold.

Or, if not cold, drunk.

We're not drunk now because we have nothing to drink.

But if we had, say, a keg of beer, we would drink that keg of beer and then we would steal that coat.

The coat hangs on a coat-rack at a nightclub too dingy to have a coat-check.

The coat is hung by its sagging shoulder.

It's a navy pea coat, heavy wool, double-breasted.

There are black buttons which, if it were our coat, we'd replace with gold buttons.

After dancing all night the cold freezes the sweat in our hair.

After dancing all night, it's not capitalism, it's communism.

Does this sound familiar?

You went back inside to get us a coat.

It wasn't until the next day that someone came banging on the door.

No amount of abuse could force us from under the duvet.

Only the abuser could – and would – if you didn't occupy the door-frame.

Newly sewn on the coat's shoulder, you pointed to your name.

Let me show you which is worse, he said, *the cold or the pain.*

5. Home

The home, you said, is our only cause.

We lived with you neither quarantined nor condemned.

We harvested root vegetables from lumpy couches where potatoes took root in loamy soil.

We sipped at mugs of thick tea steeped from mushrooms sprouting in the tub.

To be at home is not just a metaphor, you said – citing everything from inspiration to bowel movements.

We hopped with the rabbits grazing on leafy mold around skirting boards in the den.

We scraped morning cigarettes from ceiling resin and brewed beer from carpet yeast.

We held our bowels, observing nature from within.

Throughout the day, you cooked while we cleaned until we all played at puzzles, at ping-pong.

We made our own sun and shade.

We smelled of smoke and sweat, shit and sea-salt, and potpourri.

We watched our nails grow well past the quick.

Home is where the – Home is where the – Home is where the… the stereo played, over and over, our considerable conversations.

Though our door was firmly on the ground, our home floated just shy of the sky.

Remember how leaves fell inside us?

In the colors of condiments, we squeezed our night's dreams from the lazy arms of chairs.

6. *In the cold we get dark*

We're falling behind in our expectations.

We make a house out of snow.

Another word for snow is snow.

We haven't stopped talking about the snow since we got here.

Or the cold.

      Our spines are cold.

      Our dimes are cold.

      Our spines are a stack of dimes are –

Victor, we want your friendship not your money!

For so long, we've lived our life like ice, constantly melting.

How do we stop the melting?

Put the ice on ice, you said one day.

Each step has become a wish to step back.

We're walking from nowhere to no-one.

Nothing can be distinguished from something.

Who was it that said there is no disambiguation about the dark?

Our hands in front of us are dark.

Our dogs behind us are dark.

Our hands on our dogs are –

There is nothing gradual about degradation.

There is nothing gradual about affiliation.

If we had to describe our friendship – we'd say it's somewhere between *desert* and *dessert*.

Somewhere between water and land.

Something like walking on water when we can barely stand.

7. The pleasure and utility of friendship

Friendship is almost analogous to living.

But so, too, is taxidermy almost analogous to living.

We watch the twitching squirrels, the shifting moles, the fox ferrying by.

None are yet dead, not even us.

Who was it that risked death for justice?

We once found you with meningitis, curled up like a mouse on the floor.

We all peed orange for a week.

Bah to death! we said, pushing past the nurse to take our pills.

Bah to death! we say, sliding over the ice to see you now.

Doubt, like fear, is a trait best captured in the cold.

> The snow falling into our eyes – captured!

> Our embrace of you and your embrace of us – captured!

Nobody, but nobody, would choose to live without friends.

Why do you choose to live without friends? —
captured!

Our friendship is private, voluntary, and forever
happening in the distance.

We imagine the fox and the squirrel stuffed with wood
wool in a dioramic game of cards.

The fox loses his shirt, his clothes, the feelings in his toes,
while the squirrel stays warm in a second pair of socks.

'What if I need the second pair of socks? What if my own
toes get cold?'

The friendship of animals is one of utility.

Where our friendship is one of pleasure... the pleasure,
say, of a pair of seal-fur lined gloves.

We've never asked you for anything, we've just always
assumed.

And, O, how our hands are cold —

O how our hands are now cold!

8. The goodness in you

So many footfalls stepping out across the ice.

The only difference between the ice and the land is the way we slip.

We bite our lips according to plan.

                                        Because Victor:

Nobody can fall quite like we can fall.

You once lent a helping hand even when we didn't need a helping hand.

Let's get the band back together.

It's true we've called on you too many times in the past, but this isn't the past.

The goodness in you we knew the first time we licked the salt from the back of your hand.

We slammed our tequila down!

Who else offered us a lemon from his lemon tree?

Who else had an orangery?

Lemons, the size of a fist, the size of your heart –

Who else watched us vomit in the park?

We've heard that goodness can lag like the lag between lightning and thunder.

The goodness we saw in you we didn't need to hear.

A caribou runs past, like lightning after thunder.

It makes not even a whimper when the wolves pull it to the ground.

At the sound of your footsteps, we promise not even to prick up our ears.

9. *Someone once asked us what we now ask ourselves*

We tell ourselves you resemble only a feeling.

And that this feeling resembles a state of mind.

How easy would it be to replace a state of mind with a state of mind?

When we first met you, we used words like square-jawed, lanky, and dialectically hard-to-find.

Would another like you have blue or brown eyes?

Our huskies are bi-eyed – they sit on the sled staring dreamily into the distance.

The moon in our eyes is dead in the night sky.

We contemplate an appropriate exchange rate for the return of our lives.

What have you ever promised us? if anything, if ever?

The advice about the night – isn't enough to warrant this sort of devotion.

What besides us and our imaginations have you conquered?

It was without you that we mastered the art of teppanyaki: the flaming onion, a shrimp-tail flipped into our pocket as we stood over the BBQ watching butterflies of ash float by.

Who ever believed you were a BBQ Masterologist?

Or a lepidopterologist? A Hitachi Wand Vibratologist?

(Except that one time – our wives.)

What we wouldn't give to see the bright flames of wings flickering in the distance.

What we wouldn't give to turn our backs on the wind, in tangible signs of togetherness.

Those of us who think we're facing North point at those of us who think we're facing South.

In the mouth of this valley, the wind blows us open like a blouse.

10. A friend named Guy

We should have known our friendship was doomed from the moment you left us.

But our girlfriends had girlfriends with boyfriends.

And soon we had wives who knew wives with husbands named Guy.

Have we told you about Guy?

We helped Guy with a merger and an acquisition, and he represented us during an untimely scandal with a junior colleague.

He flew a stealth-bomber into Hell for us, and we project managed his L-shaped extension.

We are ten thousand miles from the heat of Hell, come to find you where you never wanted to be found.

To run is to ask us to follow you underground –

Is there nothing mutual in you?

We've had it up to the sky with you.

What would you say if we asked Guy to close the distance between sky and land for us?

What if we ask Guy – when we die – to mind our mothers and daughters, sisters and wives?

Obliging is our greatest virtue.

To oblige is as much a choice as *to-not-oblige*, just as *to walk* is as much a choice as *to-not-walk*.

We're done talking, but we've something to say.

We untuck our chins from our scarves and get sick in the snow.

We're embarrassing ourselves again, Victor, we know.

It's not so much a risk as a goal.

11. *Nothing has ever been achieved without enthusiasm*

What can we say?

Please forgive our backhandedness.

To cite another friend was more cheap than cheerful.

Our upchucking was an unimaginative moment, and the slowing down of our blood admittedly maudlin.

Friends that we are, we know you'll forgive us our friendship.

We're marching towards you with a mind even you can't control.

Without light, we can still make out the white, which gives us renewed hope and vigour.

Somebody sniggers.

But we can see the road ahead, as clearly as our hands.

Of course, it's not a road so much as more snow.

Of course, our hands are no longer our hands.

The white – the perpetual twilight – is just blue enough to see the wind fighting the wind.

Have we mentioned our dogs? They're feeling good enough to eat.

Not for *us* to eat – don't fool around!

No need to throw us a bone, Victor, we carry a sack of 'em on our backs.

No, we're not a sack of bones – don't fool around!

It's coming true: our friendly feelings for you are extensions of our friendly feelings for ourselves.

Everything is possible to overcome.

Except self-deception, self-loathing, self-love.

12. *The last time was not the last time*

On the occasion of your leaving the last time, it was not the last time.

We were neck-deep in a tournament of board games.

To capture was to preserve, but to jump was profound.

We jumped from the green grass of day into the dark woods of night.

We made mojitos and drank them outside sitting on our sofa.

Everything was moveable and drinkable, even our sofa.

We reconstituted ourselves as the jitō of Japan, and claimed the border-land of our neighbors whose back garden caught the late sun.

On the occasion of your leaving, we'd been minding our own business, had forgotten our business when we received a knock on the door, a phone call, something small.

    Have you seen —— *?*

You'd become an abstraction, the absence of something real.

You weren't the dog, a wind-chime, the apple pie we nicked from the ledge of our neighbor's open window.

It was only a matter of time before the damp of loss grew within us like moss.

We contacted the police, the CIA, the FBI.

We were working on deciphering a note written in your own cryptic hand when we were asked for a statement about intent and idolatry.

Victor, we said, he's 5' 6" or 6' 5", brown or blond hair, slight or large build, a man who can't be killed.

What did we miss most?

Your carelessness with your own life and your every possession except us.

We knew nothing about the rules of estrangement.

We knew nothing about who was on or off side.

We were still ordering oysters when you warned us of the algal bloom's red tide.

13. *So long without women*

So long without women, we're thinking of women.

There is no woman like a woman.

There is no body like our bodies.

Our melancholies.

Much is happening to us, but we cannot do anything about it.

There is a reason men go off alone, but only you know it.

When we find you, will we find you at home?

With a woman – atop or below?

We never said you denied the body for the good of the mind.

X number of women would do the X of us fine.

A stitch in time would stop the cold coming into our suits.

Under our hoods, we're thinking about the pursuit of happiness.

Are you happy? What would make us happy?

Right now, we would trade happiness for heartiness.

A hearty soup is not unheard of as the root of happiness.

We contemplate a soup of broth and noodles.

Those of us who are vegetarian, add no chicken, no pork.

Those of us who are not, feel the lack of chicken and pork.

We imagine a woman floating in our soup.

We sip at our soup even though it cannot make us happy, or hot, or homemade.

14. *There is nothing erotic about the snow*

There is nothing erotic about the snow, except for how
quickly it melts.

What we couldn't do with our hands, we made up for
with our mouths.

Until the snow was no longer cold.

Until the outside was as inside: against a tree, or laid flat
on the back of a blanket, atop the warm hood of a car.

To be under nothing, not even night.

To be blown upside down on a windy day.

We learned everything we knew from witnessing you.

Wrapped in the legs of Alexis: into the marrow of her long bones,
you dipped your spoon.

She fell in a swoon.

It's astronomical, she said. The moon.

Cocooned for a week, you fed on oranges and dates, the
blue cheese we hate.

How else could we emulate but by watching?

You with Jess and Tess, and Steph and Max.

We never confessed what you knew to be true: we gave
the ax to Jax.

She chopped down your door when we went to the store
for more ink.

We'd been working on perfecting our chop marks for a
month.

Our calligraphy was amateur at best, but we wouldn't
rest.

We signed into constitution our diagrams of you giving
144 different types of heightened response.

When you plugged the hole in your ceiling, it was as if we
were circumcised a second time, un-anesthetized.

15. Let us tell you about our wives

Let us tell you about our wives.

Together we were spectators of late night minor ops:
        breast implants,   meniscus tears,
        the removal of   pre-malignant moles.

One mole grew laterally, until it took the irregular shape
of this Arctic space across the map of her back.

We saw the hole in the ice.

We saw the hole we'd have in our life –
        took the babysitter to the children,
        held her hand as our wife.

We're only joking! It was day, not even night!

We made dinner while our wives paid the bills.

They took out the trash, while we bathed the kids.

On Tuesday-night TV, we ogled together a pretty girl
slaying vampires.

On Thursdays, our wives let us bite their necks when we
became vampires ourselves.

One wife tore her meniscus in training for a triathlon –
        we fingered her arthroscopic scars.

One had breast implants –
        we did a face-plant in her décolletage.

Our wives let us kick and field.

Sometimes they fielded what we kicked –
    (& vice versa).

Life... was not all that bad – we never said life was all that bad.

To keep the home running smoothly requires some give and take, some see and saw.

We see-sawed with our kids in the park.

(We'll come later to our kids in the park).

On Fridays, we went to *Fridays*, occasionally *Trattoria Alfredo.*

After, we went to see Leonardo DiCaprio.

Leonard DiCaprio may be the finest actor of his generation, but he was not born to play the parts we were born to play.

We could have been airline moguls – without the money, or the sense of adventure, or the women.

We could have been cops, who pretended to get kicked out of the cops, who wooed the gangster cop's woman.

On the way home, we did it with our wives in the car.

Pulled over into the woods, our wives astride us in the car.

By the lake, we did it twice. On the way home, thrice in the car.

Despite everything, our wives rarely made us say please.

Our beards are too heavy with ice to blow like they used to blow in the breeze.

16. Clear plastic raincoat

Out of the white steps a woman in a clear plastic raincoat.

Why is she wearing a clear plastic raincoat when it's not even raining?

We might think she wears it in anticipation of rain but more plausibly it's to declare: *I've nothing to hide.*

Our guess is she does have something to hide.

That sort of openness – exhibitionist, fetishist – is twice as deliberate as a flasher's... an invitation to see who she really is, but to test our imaginations as well.

The man she's talking to looks like death on a soda cracker.

Theirs is the sort of relationship that will only ever be consummated by murder.

She's laughing now as if she's just been splashed by a puddle.

It's a question of motives: what is she doing with him?

And if he is rich, does that make her a gold digger?

The clear plastic raincoat may say she is not a gold digger, but it also says, *Take me home, I'm sweaty and matted underneath.*

Don't look now, but she's removing her raincoat.

If this were happening at 23° latitude, instead of 83°
latitude, we would help her to take it off her shoulder.

And she would offer us a smile.

And on that smile we would buggy over the dunes,
through the sun and the surf, the sand and the seaweed:

        − until we were tan and lean
        − until we were equatorial
        − until the waters turned boreal.

17. The lingering hours of late morning

What about the lingering hours of late morning?

How do we occupy so many of them?

In the mornings, we lingered over our wives' toes.

In the mornings, we lingered over the sounds made by the couple in the apartment below.

We've always known our lives were finite, but we didn't recognize it until we got this close to the end.

There was nothing ever profound in us, and yet here we are, with something profound in us.

We'd rather be found dead in a polar bear than alive in khakis and button-downs, boat shoes instead of snowshoes on casual day.

On casual day, we used to arrive late into work after reading the paper and drinking coffee with the woman we loved.

What's so great about, Victor? our beloved would ask.

But to ask was to know:

Work *may be* living. Loving *may be* living.

But friends like us will always seek each other, whatever the weather.

We loosen our stride, imagine the calm before the clam bake.

Honey, we're home, we used to say.

Our kids would jump into our arms, our dogs would bark into our arms.

Somewhere, everywhere, people are finding each other.

The sun may not be shining on them, but we are looking towards the horizon as if it were.

18. *Fata Morgana*

In the distance, wearing a sombrero, half-buried in snow,
we suddenly see Victor.

One can circle the globe looking for a friend, but here
you've been all along, donning a hat of come-hither hints
and half-formed suggestions – a beacon for polar birds of
supernatural agencies.

The air below us is colder than the air above, and in all
your superior complexity you stand with hands
outstretched, floating above the ice.

A flock of pure white willow ptarmigan circle you.

Bubo scandiacus barks: *krek-krek*!

We are so happy we feel the need to knock the hood off
the person in front of us.

Victor, you're so bright, you've become a reflection of the
sky – an unseasonable, not-an-unreasonable occurrence.

We're feeling again the turbulence of moving towards
you as you move away from us.

Victor: elevated, then lowered,
shortened, then stretched,

as large as a constellation in the sky, and the
same unreliable number of miles away.

We can no longer see the fun in wearing the wrong head-
wear for the wrong season.

We'd try you Victor for treason if there weren't an
attractive young woman standing by your side.

> *Your friend,* she says, *is an allegory for a star, a life
> choice for those of us who've lost our voice.*

It warms us to ask for a date.

When she turns her head to the sun, we blame the cold
for the intimacy of our squeeze.

> *Victor vibrates.*
> *Victor speeds.*
> *Victor's coming right for us!*

We separate and flutter, stretch, then compress, till you
disappear, lost again in the atmosphere.

In this world, we know a mirage when we see one.

But we don't doubt what we don't see.

We walk looking down at our shoes.

In the ice we spy your sombrero like a truss-headed
screw.

19. Sans women, qua men

What is typical of you is not typical of us.

What do men do *qua* men?

Because you are here, we are here, does not follow.

Let us for once:

> buy you a beer,
> lean nonchalantly on your garden gate,
> double date.

One of us proposes: *It is reasonable to suppose that those who don't search have a more pleasant life than those who do.*

And yet we search nonetheless.

We imagine you in the summer, sweating by the pool, wrapped in white fur, bouncing atop the 10-meter board ready to dive below.

Who did you know that we never knew?

Because you dive, we dive doesn't follow.

We want a hot dish, not *ceviche*.

We want bolognaise, not mayonnaise.

We'd trade our street cred for some breadcrumbs, swap spit for pricked thumbs.

There is no blood between us, don't even try to wash it off your hands.

We remember the Bangwa of Cameroon –

according to whom, you were assigned to us at noon.

The hour of our birth, for what it's worth.

20. *If we had a map*

From up here, we can almost see where we've been coming from.

We'd be off the map altogether, if we had a map.

If we had a map, we still wouldn't know how to get back.

Tap, we say with our boots on the ice. *Tap-tap, tap.*

To the explorers before us, we say we never meant to go exploring.

We never wanted to know the unknown.

Our lack of ambition was in our lack of attitude.

We dissed the converging of longitudes.

The longitudes have converged to this point where time is irrelevant.

But nothing is irrelevant.

Not us, not the sharks we imagine below us.

Latitudes circle us like sharks.

It would take some serious maths to compute the depths of our frostbite.

How many mega-bites of ice would it take to get us home?

If we had a virtual car, we'd put virtual chains around its virtual wheels.

With each step we take, we spin our wheels.

We're driving into all the time zones in all the world.

We watch our kids waking up, our boss staking up, our wives taking their place in this world without us.

Everything is south from here, even the light.

Everything is white from here, even the sea.

We poke a hole looking for some life on the other side of the world.

If we had a map, we'd twist it into a swan or a swan-boat.

With each step we've taken, the world has gotten bigger and bigger.

Our thumbprints are as big as our footprints.

With each step we take, the angle of tilt gets demanding.

What rotation of axis is needed to turn us home?

We have no passports and invite remanding.

II.

21. Where the light becomes the land

There is nothing gradual about the light.

It's as sudden as overnight, after six months of overnight.

It comes bubbling up like a spring where there are no springs.

When you're all the time in the dark you forget about the dark, until the white gets white.

Until the light is ice.

Until the light is a bright crack in our bones.

We crack a bleached-white caribou bone and look through it toward home.

In the distance, the black of the rock ridges meets the black of the cliffs.

In the distance, are the remaining stones of subterranean homes.

We crawl inside what's left like a crab.

We've developed the cool habits of the landscape.

We don't need much, we don't eat much, we don't sleep much.

When did we change from guests to residents?

When did the sea-ice become the ground-ice?

When did our walking on ice become our walking on land?

We've stopped wondering about safe ice or unsafe ice, safe light or unsafe light.

Lying in the snow, we take the shape of snow.

Looking up at the clouds, we take the shape of clouds.

We stand to take a bow.

Don't ask us why, or to whom, or how.

22. The path

The sea is melting into floes.

The melt-water softens our dogs' paws and ice splinters their toes.

We tie seal-skin boots they try to flick off.

We sled the ice-foot, the belt of shore-fast, until the air is as crass as the water below.

The ground is patched brown like our faces.

We stand with knees tucked, bent-backed until the wind blows thin willows slack against the sky.

Who is happier than us to be alive?

It's easy to see the copse as a corpse – but trees are trees.

Give us breath or give us death!

We struggle through the willows till they become the pines we've had in our mind for some time.

Snow mixes with dirt – bare-black.

The mountains behind us slip away flat-packed.

We walk a path of flowers pale and pink until we hear Victor, in the trees, ready to fall like snow.

Under our feet the flowers crack, blue as glass.

Under our feet, the dogs circle, the shadows of birds
flash.

A change in the wind is a change in our luck.

Uncovered: a rusty chainsaw, an orange...

23. The path, continued

                                 ... truck.

The path in front of us is part muck, part shuck of engines.

A two-stroke engine with a problem confronts us.

We can't fix a two-stroke anymore than we can fix a four-stroke.

A wet spark plug, someone says, can mean many things.

A wet dream, we say, can mean many things.

The sparks look lost, weak, slack-jawed.

The path doesn't crash – but it has a weak chin, a smash-through-the-windshield sort-of-grin.

We'd smile if it didn't hurt.

From over our shoulders one of our huskies lolls a tongue black as oil:

        Check the ground wire for the ignition coil.

The gas line sprays and we're on our knees praying for a spark.

A path is its own catheter.

Rewire the hope in our hearts with the veins in our legs.

Any minute now, Victor, we expect you to step out of the
fog like one of our dogs with a wrench, whacking pistons:

> *tick*
>
> > *tick*

> *ping!*

We're high on the smell of smoke that fills the sky.

Not from behind, but ahead.

Burning dwarf willow and heather, from a camp above
the weather.

24. *We come on the back of snowmobiles*

We come on the back of snowmobiles.

We come on the backs of whales.

If not whales, ships; if not ships, planes.

We explain we've no interest in fame or adventure.

We're not missionaries nor settlers with a cough.

Five families in five huts welcome us with meat up from
the meat-holes.

Seal fat: white as ice and more slippery.

> To your health! we say. May your nose be as cold
> and your feet as warm as Victor's: *Tee-toi-te!*

Walrus: carved thin and rare and spread with a fat not
unlike the horseradish cream we've been craving in our
dreams.

> To your wealth! May you find on your land, the
> gold and oil of Victor: *Tee-toi-te!*

On a platter of ice: the murre eggs of sea birds, low flying
auklets, boiled and stored in seal oil, the dovekies
fermented like very ripe brie.

> You can tell Victor by his stare – we stare – like a
> bear: More *tee-toi-te*, please!

We slurp jigged tomcod and sculpins in a seaweed soup,
pick our teeth with the spindly legs of crabs, before
trying to hail a cab:

Take a right at the light, double back, and drop us
at the corner of Victor's!

Pushed to the sides of our plates, we leave behind cloud
berries and spring greens, roots and willow shoots, a
salad of Kamchatka rock cress, sour mountain sorrel and
wallflower, seaweed and sea-leaves.

If only you were Victor, are the last words we hear, when
we're laid down – to melt with the ice all around.

25. Caribou

Perspective: what is our perspective?

Above and below, and everything in between.

From where we're lying, we could lie happily forever:

> on a platform of dense mats of willow twigs tied
> with seal thong;

> over which, moose hide and bear skin, five feet
> wide;

> over which, soft as a chamois, two girls we call
> Tammy;

> under deep-pile caribou hide.

Victor, we can see by the glint in their eyes, that Tanaraq
and Tarralikitak have met you:

> they've roses bursting from their cheeks.
> and more roses tucked behind their ears.

Their husbands and fathers are out hunting the caribou
we earlier pantomimed without satisfaction.

Despite our hands held high in the shape of antlers, our
backs arched flat, we arose suspicion in our fire-
coloured, faux-fur trimmed coats.

Nobody spooks like a caribou spooks.

Except us, when our kids jump on our backs despite our bad backs.

Thank you for the adjustments Tanaraq and Tarralikitak, we're feeling just fine.

Under this igloo's roof of ice, we crack like a glacier through the core.

Our colonial lore.

26.

The blue-green light through the ice gives the impression
of sky-height.

Our faces have been burnt sun-black.

We prepare an unguent of subcutaneous ptarmigan fat.

Tammy and Tammy, we say, how about a game of strip-
tac-toe?

And because the break in our nose and the shape of our
eyes reminds them of you, Victor, we're all of us half-way
down to our skin when the hunters come in.

Before we disgrace you further, consider appearing
before we disappear.

This blackmail isn't emotional – it's devotional.

In the flight for the door, we pull out pictures of our kids playing
in the park.

Hiding in the tree's leaves, our wives too can be seen.

> *Even you* – you see – *see.*

For a moment, there's the swell of sympathy in T & T's
eyes.

Long after we're thrown out the door, we implore:

Tell us where to find Victor and we won't bother you anymore!

We're not fit to be father or brother, husband or lover.

The men point us in one direction, the women another.

27. *In stars, in cars, in Mars*

We've stopped believing in stars, in cars, in Mars.

Stars are as dead to us as warmth and light.

Nothing is real: not the white, not the cold.

We lost consciousness long ago.

The North Star could only lead us so far into knowing who we are.

Our limitations are measured in exhalations.

    Sigh.

How could you not know this would happen?

Unless... you always knew this would happen?

Victor, you're as sly as the polar bear tracking us!

Your test of us is a test of our conscience.

You can smell us from a mile away.

Don't run yet, Victor, let us find you first.

Your test of us is a test of our Orientalism –

      How far away is our Orientalism?

If you're not in front of us, you must be behind us.

Looking for us in a car, Mars, a star.

In our backyards, we telescoped to the stars.

Telescoping was like eloping – with someone else's wife,
silhouetted behind the blinds.

It's a way to keep the love alive.

> *To lie*
> > *down alive.*

Much as we try, our best thoughts no longer sound
better coming from you.

28. Notwithstanding the rejection we've suffered

Notwithstanding the rejection we've suffered, we never minded much about the dark.

Now that the light surrounds us, we can say that it was in the dark we felt closest to you.

All we know and have known, we could write on the back of an ice-cube – (about *absence*, about *want*).

In the absence of you, we're naming this floe, Joe.

Atop Joe, we tell you about our glacial ambitions, our love of fresh water, our need to stand upon (and be stood upon), broken-backed – until we get to where we've always wanted to go.

For this lift to shore, for the shelter of the sheer edge, we're still frozen but no longer freezing.

In the dusky light of day, we're keeping it liturgical.

After so much dark, we're feeling allergic to light.

We recall once finding you lost in the half-light breaking through the blinds.

One of us fumbled with the switch.

> *Lights please*, you said.

One of us fumbled with the switch.

Lights please, you said again.

The brightness that befell us quelled us into a brief
moment of wisdom by which we could see you seeing us.

Not on, you said, *Off.*

One of us coughed.

29. Panegyric

Who will respond to the nostalgia of men like us?

Victor, come to us upon this zephyr with your weapons cocked.

We admit our festschrift was only ever half-hearted.

But our tongues might as well be pulled from an *aglu* and thumped upon the ice for all the empathy they incite.

Only a head as heavy as yours could withstand our cries of pain.

We invite you to claim our souls with your hands, to give us something that'll go viral on video.

To give a beating is one thing, but to take blow-by-blow requires the sort of inner-strength that's ours alone.

Without you, we imagine daily our enemies approaching us from the distance.

> *Heaven-help-us* breaks out across our chests in hives.

> *Heaven-help-us* our wives tattoo on their inner thighs.

If we had a boom box, we'd blast some heavy rap from the safety of a widow's walk, while you rise up from the powder to appear in front of us with a pea-shooter.

Oh! smite the agitators in the V of their open-necked
shirts, exposing creamy-throats!

Even though their breath is stifled, out squeaks a joke:

Have you heard the one about the man who left the
world behind to live alone on snow-cones, to watch
from his look-out for a cook-out that might start a
forest fire where there are no forests?

What right do we have to be idolatrous, we ask you in
smoke signals.

Who are we to be telling tales of *you*?

Come to us this Winter, like Spring.

30. Antarctic enemies

Your enemies are our enemies it goes without saying.

Yet how close we have come to resembling the enemy.

The trouble with the enemy is the trouble with the Earth's axis of rotation.

The Earth's axis asks us to stand opposite wherever you stand.

And wherever you stand, the sea-depth dictates – simply – murkiness.

Cut through the sea ice: cut through the Earth's core to the Antarctic.

In the Antarctic, it's more black than white, more rock than snow...

The sheerness two-times us into a cuckold with vertigo.

Each peak greets us like a beholding.

Each peak shows us light is more about flight than illumination.

In the Antarctic, we find a variant enemy with a variant side.

And he's got an ax to grind.

(After-which, you don't want to be found alive.)

We are not diametrically opposed to anything in this
world, except separation: from our arms and legs,
hearts and minds.

Watch your wrists in the Antarctic, or the anti-Victor will
grab your hand and expose your cubital fossa.

He knows not to bleed you dry.

If this were sci-fi, we'd mutate and multiply.

31. *It's more physical than philosophical*

We never asked you to like us.

Or to *be* like us.

We'd dismiss this friendship on the grounds of
inequality, if we weren't saying your name daily.

We're studying hard the cracks in the clouds, neglecting
the cracks in the ice.

To fall into you would be twice-as-nice.

To be hypothermic in less than a minute, sinking down
below the ice with the seals.

To be without breath would be like breathing to us.

We know there's a finer point to be made than you.

We know the ground is the sky times two.

It's more physical than philosophical.

Our curse is to learn how *not* to die.

What we'd give to be stuck in formaldehyde.

To exchange ice for fire.

To exchange wet for dry.

There are so many reasons why our beards have gone white, and none include snow.

If we had a razor, we'd shave.

If we had a mirror, we'd wave.

There's a tool we brought with us, just in case we can't find our way back – made of metal and gin, bullets and smack, a black plastic sack.

We're hanging the last of our hope on our soap-on-a-rope.

32. Time

Don't get down, we tell ourselves –

> not on this side of town! – not when we've so
> much time left.

Downtown, there was a watch shop where we spent too
much time browsing and not enough time contemplating
the positive attitudes of men who died in the snow.

From our offices, we'd walk the two blocks looking up at
the sun and the moon, until we asked for their removal as
horological markers.

We've given up studying the hands of our hand-wound
minute repeater, tourbillion-powered chronograph in a
skeleton case.

Through its sapphire crystal, we can no longer see
ourselves shoveling sidewalks.

Before we sealed the deal, we smiled at the sales-lady
and she raised the price, citing the fluctuation of gold.

But this is not gold, we said – and we put our hands up
her shirt.

And she put her hands up our shirt – to feel the beating of
our heart… a tale of false starts.

Time looms in units we can no longer measure.

An accuracy of +/- a day every day.

In case of emergency, our watch came with a flare.

We set it off the day we set out, over cabernet and camembert.

33. On the occasion of finding others like us

The embarrassment of our search would be even more embarrassing if we didn't come across others as embarrassed.

Men like us: stumbling, frost-bitten-black, with plastic bags over shoes, snow melting down backs.

We're about to challenge them to a contest of commitment, when we see the yellow of mustard around their mouths, and the gunk of Chapstick in their eyes.

They're shaking just to keep the pulse in their pulse.

We'd offer them a hot dog if we had a hot dog.

Our dogs share with their dogs the remains of nothing.

The rapture that comes with starving we rate about an eight out of ten.

Their temples beat where their skulls have gone thin.

With no water, ecstasy comes in fits.

We'd always thought this trip un-shareable not just unbearable.

> *Drink*, we say, as if we have anything to drink.

> How long, they say, since you've heard any-thing, of any-body?

We tell the tale of getting lucky in Massachusetts only to be gonnorheic by Duluth.

From the doctor's table, we watched Victor hanging off a ferris wheel, practicing loop-de-loops.

34. Cows

With the horizon all around us, all eyes are on the man
who wanders off alone.

Dotting the white with their black and white, he sees
cows on this floe.

The cow in these men's eyes is a glow even we don't
know.

> *He was the back end of a cow at the state-fair: blue
> ribbon, five years running.*

What we wouldn't give for the cold white milk of a cow,
though we've never milked anything in our lives.

When our wives took out a breast we were always
surprised.

The cow in these men's eyes is big and brown and iced-
over where it used to be teary.

We're no good at consoling, or controlling our emotions
or fears.

We sleep standing, till we fall:

> tipped by the man who's returned for some cow-
> tipping.

Not finding is not failure, he says, and he turns:

> toward the sea as green as a pasture –

toward a pasture on which there's a pier –

toward a ship – like a cow – sailing so near.

35. A prepared state of bonhomie

Even without you Victor, we're beginning to believe in something unbelievable.

Every road-trip ends with the hope of a boat.

We're about to run into the water, to splash like we once splashed in a tub full of ice during an especially high fever.

In anticipation of being hauled aboard, we pull our ripcords.

But these men we're with:

> Why the long faces and undone laces?

We hurry past them to short and quick conclusions.

Starboard is not for everyone.

And neither are we.

In our prepared state of bonhomie –

> against a backdrop of snow-fall,

> against the sea's swell –

> from a hillock to the deck below.

When the ship's horn blows, we blow solo.

36. E.

It turns out we were standing in line in T. – formerly
known as A. – when we meet E.

We're enjoying being led – it's like a shock to the head.

It's just E.'s sort of get-up-and-go that we need to get-up-
and-go *with*.

Sure, it's wet and it's cold, but you don't see E. sitting
by the fire waiting for a knock on the door to begin her
tour.

Victor calls to you, she says. *Friends call to you* – in a place
where you can wash your beards and your minds in
warm, mineral-rich, milky-blue waters.

We're on a narrow long boat on a long narrow strait.

The fish are bigger than the waves are bigger than the
fish.

We're about to get sick when the land comes quicker
than the sky ever did.

From boat to bus, we cross the green and black, the
moss-covered volcanic brack.

The rain brings more rain, until the water runs off the
windshield in an image of E: paddle-headed and pony-tailed.

Harbinger!

We're tired of Time, and Want, and Danger, and
our Infinite Remoteness.

Tell us we no longer need to walk alone.

Put your pedal to the metal and promise us someday
we'll exchange names.

37. *The nightlife is the right life for us*

This town has been waiting for us.

We enter it under bunting and a parade.

Rumour has reached us – has reached-*out* to us.

We're served the customary meat soup of winter even though it's summer.

The Arctic chill that burns our feet and lightens our heads is gone.

Our credit cards have been cancelled and our checks won't clear.

Your money's no good here, someone says.

We're bought a beer, and a beer, and another beer.

We're jumping like reindeer on the dance-floor, when we hear we can't dance for *shhh* –.

We take off our pants.

Time to go, says E., who ushers us off stage with the promise of a shower and a shave.

> *E., don't get us wrong, in your lime-colored wool*
> *and water-colored eyes, you're the best surprise*
> *going, but the love we bear –*

A long, song-like sleep, she says.

Our hotel is a small but grand affair, with a view of the city and the sky.

There's a mix of the hip and the corporate and we don't just stand out because we stink.

We register as *Searching-for-Victor, inc.*

It's the anonymity we like best when we lock the door and fall asleep on the floor.

A grey sky is soon a dark-blue sky is soon a white, cloud-filled sky that's pink.

A light so bright even at night breaks through the glass.

In the morning, we wake to E. outside our window fixing our window.

38. The day-tour

E., how can we expect you to understand our expectations?

We've only just hopped on your hop-on/hop-off tour and already we're sighing.

It's not that the stretch of road past the Lobster House and the National Gallery (on our left), the city pond (on our right) – is boring, but do you find it boring?

We urge you to consider that we can't start what we haven't yet stopped.

It's no longer in our nature to sit when we can stand.

Just like it's not in our nature to stand when we can walk.

How can we just switch off?

These are questions for the farm land on the adjacent peninsula.

We chase each other into a church nave until we resemble the devout.

8 stained glass windows tell the deep red and blue story of spread and settlement – of popularity and pursuit – of those friends we have the least control of but want to control all the more:

Wounds from a friend can be trusted,
but an enemy multiplies kisses.

We drive back through the farm land, past a lone blue
corrugated house with corrugated metal roof, a single
room with windows on each side, and a reflection in the
water that surrounds with silver and brown, the
white wash of the sky.

We drive through the fishing village where we watch the
trawlers deposit their catch of herring and haddock and
cod.

We swim in the community swimming pool until we're as
clean as we are sober.

We drive past a strip mall and a former TB hospital now
over-looking a pond of arctic char, brown trout, eel and
tiddler.

The sky is changing from mottled blue to ice white, mist
and fog, snow-capped mountains in the faraway distance
across the water.

We swim with the salmon in the river that runs the
motorway back into town, through industrial estates and
container terminals, down to the valleys where we do
our laundry next to the bronze sculpture of a woman
doing her laundry.

We pass the football stadium and the handball stadium,
where Presidential candidates have battled it out.

We don't mean to get political, but we've forgotten where
we stand on the disappearance of borders and people?

We're undecided about national pride – was Victor ever a spy?

E., we can't see our friend for these missing trees in these absent woods.

Standing by the waterside is a house of national romanticism but it isn't our *romanticism*.

We're feeling the after-effects of unseasonable apathies, wit, and animal wishes pulling us away from the land we've just landed in.

A spirit hovers over the chess matches being played in the square and resides in the church's pipe organ.

A spirit walks along the coast, past the impressive new concert hall emanating green, futuristic light from the green futuristic cubes of glass.

A spirit comes to us in the old harbor, with its shi-shi restaurants and artisan shops, its whale-watching ships docked on the left, and whale-catching ships docked on the right.

No E., we don't want a whale-watching tour.

Unless our friend has taken that whale-watching tour?

We want this statue of the founding fathers to be, in Victor's parlance, *suited and booted.*

We want a hotdog at this world-famous hotdog stand.

The man at the stand offers us a hotdog with a thin line of mustard.

No thanks, E. says, they'll have what I'm having: a dog with everything on it: ketchup and remoulade, fried onions and raw onions, brown, bitter mustard and sweet, pepper mustard – all slathered with red relish.

Oh E., let us take your whale-watching tour.

39. The commiseration of whale watchers

Whale-watchers, we do not want to hear about your afternoon squinting into the light.

We know only too well how heartache comes at the end of a tour.

Let your knees give into the sea-sickness that comes after seeing no whales.

There is no solace in the epiphanies one experiences alone along the way.

Whale-watchers, do not let your guide offer you consolation in the sky.

The light which breaks through the clouds… is *not* fantastic.

The clouds which break up the blue… are *not* fantastic.

From the vantage point of your boat upon the water, you can only see more water.

Even if the waves share the shape of a whale, they are *not* a whale.

Meditation and contemplation won't make it any better.

A whale needs to come to you before it can *be*-come.

There is no comfort in knowing what is just beyond or below.

Do not offer us your commiseration.

Do not try to convince us with your hands and your hope.

It's a distortion of your true feelings, a mirage made out of more colors than the sea contains.

If nature is truly fleeting, then in its fleetingness are the limitations of our imaginations.

An absence can remain an absence until the absence of time.

It is the same euphoria that comes from starvation or fever.

Do not ask us to unroll the wet of your upturned cuffs.

Touch our foreheads, take our temperature.

Mourn.

40. It's time to come clean

It's time to come clean.

We wanted a bed and a bath and for someone else to do
the imaginary math which allowed us to pretend for just
a little while longer that we were still out there
searching.

There is nothing noble left in us.

No arch in our instep, no cleft in our chin (blown cleftless
in the wind).

We can't put our finger on just where or when we
decided to follow you – (from the moment we saw you).

Was it us or you, whistling and humming, as if we'd
never heard of words?

Was it us or you who tattooed their whole back with a
map, as if we'd never heard of navigation or
triangulation?

As if we'd never heard of Victor.

E., when you first met us, were we white or black, of man
or woman, *this* time or *that* time?

Come clean with us in this swimming pool and we'll come
cleaner with you.

We don't blame you.

Everybody needs tourists for a tour.

Tell us Victor didn't learn to knit his own scarf
or listen to a man play accordion in his home.

We have no taste for truffle and tarragon oil, or dill and
lemon oil.

We've enjoyed whiling away our days at the laundromat-
café, but we can no longer linger in your bookshops.

Your delicious cold milk will have to stay in your cold
cows.

No more dancing, nor fine-dining on your organic and
locally-produced foods.

No more house parties at your friends where our
portraits are continually painted.

We never looked so good: clothed nor naked.

41.

Nothing surprises us anymore, not even our own
surprising feelings.

It's a regressive sort of attack to want to go back to the
ice and the snow.

We pick up our pick-axes, put on our boots, scarfs and
ear-flap hats, neon coats with pockets full of cheap
smokes.

When you drop us off at the tree-line, time complicates
space:

> and already, we're halfway up the mouth of the
> glacier, where the ice is lumps and rents, and
> holes which spiral down into the unknown;
>
> and already, we're lifting our feet high enough
> to spike our crampons into the ice of our dreams,
> where we're slipping and skating up-and-down
> and around each other in figure eights.

Our last great mistake was starting off too late, and
even now the night is playing tricks on our highs and
goodbyes.

> Even now, even you E. are
> giving up your opposition
> to this onward mission.

Even now, we know it's
only the wind whispering
the name *Victor* into our
ears, like a mnemonic:

cold light

wet   *wind*

dark snow.

There is nothing to reach –
no peak nor valley.

We've run out of reasons
to tally our steps.

They're just steps.

42. *After us*

We're trading our ballpoints for the flight feathers of
large birds – swans and geese, plucked from the left wing.

For the ink, we're boiling bearberry, mixed with bare
willow twigs and peat.

Victor, we're replacing this story of you with this story of
us.

Atop this mountain, we're leaving behind

                                                    footsteps
                              clothing
          mud

                                        blood
          bone
                    soul

We're intent on becoming a new possibility – an ideology,
a collegiate body – set and settled on the principle that
what is lost will always be found…

          even if covered by wind and snow, ash and ice,
          sun and moon.

At the last minute, we refuse to disappear too soon.

We tweet this on our smart phones – before we throw
away our smart phones.

Victor, did we ever tell you – before this all began – we thought we saw you?

We were in a supermarket with our kids, sent out by our wives to buy a bagful of booze to celebrate the most wonderful news.

We were halfway out the door, when security nabbed us and embarrassed us with questions about friendship, and recycling, and our political views on the unidentified man with the blue backpack who was last spotted in aisle ten.

Not finding is not failure

(crackled over the PA)

Not finding is not failure

(said a woman dispensing paper cups of diced cheese).

So far away, it's hard not to cast our eyes to the sky where we now watch planes landing daily.

Whatever happened to the wilderness of you, to your empty space?

Whatever we can wing we can still win, our old coach used to say, before calling the final play.

We understand the promise of a call-out, a bail-out, that a newly balanced, cantilevered life, requires the sort of landing that one must do standing on their head.

We're standing on our head on a cliff edge when a
plane comes crashing down – wings snapped off,
wheels rolling past the transposed fuselage.

Everyone is alighting from somewhere.

Accidents are not the same as adventures

(the pilot announces)

Accidents are not the same as adventures

(a passenger screams).

These blown-out windows

that cock-pit

baggage

whose hold-all is this? –

We roll with men on fire in the snow.

This story of us has already become a story of others
setting out after us.

Friends

– if you must –

Lightning Source UK Ltd.
Milton Keynes UK
UKOW02f0156040915

258000UK00002B/23/P